JADA PINKETT SMITH

The Iconic Biography of Hollywood Global Superstar and the Creator of the Red Table Talk series.(Author of "Worthy")

By

ICONIC PRESS

CONTENTS

INTRODUCTION

Iconic Biography of Jada Pinkett Smith offers you a deeply personal and introspective look into the life and career of one of Hollywood biggest actress, Jada Pinkett Smith who is on a life journey of self-discovery. With meticulous research and thrilling narration, this book takes readers on a captivating exploration of her experiences, triumphs, and challenges.

In this captivating biography, delve into the extraordinary journey of Jada Pinkett Smith, from her humble beginnings to becoming a true Hollywood icon. Uncover the untold stories behind Jada's rise to fame and the incredible challenges she faced along the way.

From her early days in Baltimore to her breakthrough role in the hit television series "A Different World," Jada's path to success was anything but easy. Through sheer determination and unwavering passion, she defied the odds and carved out a place for herself in the entertainment industry.

Gain unparalleled insight into Jada's groundbreaking work as an actress, producer, and advocate for diversity and inclusion. Discover how she has fearlessly shattered stereotypes and pushed boundaries, paving the way for future generations of actors and actresses.

But this biography is not just about Jada's professional achievements. It delves deep into her personal struggles and triumphs, revealing the moments that have shaped her into the resilient woman she is today. From navigating complex relationships to overcoming self-doubt, Jada's journey is one of resilience and empowerment.

Discover Jada's true tale, including her personal life and power couple marriage with fellow American actor Will Smith, and her legendary friendship and inspirations with the late Tupac Shakur.

Jada Pinkett Smith's consistent commitment to utilize her platform for good is one of the most remarkable elements of her life. Investigate the several ways she has empowered women and campaigned for mental health awareness. Jada's influence extends far beyond the silver screen, from her revolutionary discussion program "Red Table Talk" to her involvement in many humanitarian organizations.

This biography is a must-read for anyone who wants to celebrate Jada Pinkett Smith's legacy and understand her ongoing influence on the entertainment industry. With its compelling storytelling and in-depth research, it provides an intimate look into the life of a true trailblazer. Prepare to be inspired by Jada's resilience, passion, and unwavering dedication to making a difference in the world.

You can't afford to miss out on this captivating exploration of one of Hollywood's most iconic figures. Whether you're a fan of Jada Pinkett Smith or simply interested in the stories behind the scenes, this biography will leave you inspired and in awe of her incredible journey.

It's time to explore. We wish you Happy Reading!

CHAPTER 1

EARRLY LIFE AND BACKGROUND

Family and Upbringing

Jada Pinkett Smith was born on September 18, 1971, in Baltimore, Maryland. She grew up in a working-class neighborhood, where she experienced both the challenges and opportunities that came with her environment. Pinkett Smith's family background and cultural influences played a significant role in shaping her early life.

She was born into a loving and supportive family. Her mother, Adrienne Banfield-Jones, worked as a nurse, while her father, Robsol Pinkett Jr., ran a construction company. Despite their modest means, Pinkett Smith's parents instilled in her the values of hard work and education.

Pinkett Smith's mother played a significant role in shaping her early life. She was heavily involved in the arts and recognized her daughter's talent and passion for performing from a young age. To nurture this talent, she enrolled Pinkett Smith in dance classes and exposed her to various art forms. This early exposure to the arts not only ignited Pinkett Smith's passion for performing but also instilled in her a deep appreciation for creativity and self-expression.

Growing up in a working-class neighborhood presented its own set of challenges for Pinkett Smith. The community was plagued by violence and drugs, which posed obstacles to her personal growth and development. However, she refused to let these circumstances define her and instead used them as motivation to succeed.

Despite the challenges she faced, Pinkett Smith's family provided a stable and nurturing environment. They supported her dreams and encouraged her to pursue her goals. Their belief in her abilities gave her the confidence to overcome any obstacles that came her way.

Pinkett Smith's upbringing also played a significant role in shaping her values and beliefs. Her parents emphasized the importance of hard work, education, and resilience. These values became the foundation upon which she built her successful career in the entertainment industry.

Education was particularly important to Pinkett Smith's family. They believed that it was the key to unlocking opportunities and achieving success. With this belief instilled in her, Pinkett Smith excelled academically and attended the Baltimore School for the Arts, a prestigious performing arts high school. It was during her time at this school that she honed her acting skills and gained recognition for her talent.

Jada Pinkett Smith's early life was marked by a combination of challenges and opportunities. Her family's support, her exposure to the arts, and her own determination paved the way for her successful career in the entertainment industry. Despite the obstacles she faced, Pinkett Smith's resilience and talent have made her an iconic figure in the world today.

In summary, Jada Pinkett's family and upbringing played a crucial role in shaping her early life and career. Her parents' support, her exposure to the arts, and the values they instilled in her have been instrumental in her journey towards becoming one of Hollywood's most respected and influential figures. Despite the challenges she faced, Pinkett Smith's resilience, talent, and strong family foundation have paved the way for her remarkable success.

Education and Career Beginnings

Jada Pinkett Smith's education and career beginnings were marked by her passion for performing, her dedication to her craft, and her determination to succeed in the entertainment industry.

Pinkett Smith's love for performing was evident from a young age. Her mother recognized her talent and enrolled her in dance classes to nurture her skills. This early exposure to the arts sparked Pinkett Smith's passion for performing and set her on a path towards a career in entertainment.

To further develop her talents, Pinkett Smith attended the Baltimore School for the Arts, a prestigious performing arts high school. It was during her time at this school that she honed her acting skills and gained recognition for her talent. She received critical acclaim for her performances in school productions and caught the attention of casting directors and agents.

After graduating from high school, Pinkett Smith made the bold decision to move to Los Angeles to pursue a professional acting career. Armed with her family's support and her own determination, she embarked on auditions for various roles in television and film. While initially facing rejection and setbacks, Pinkett Smith persevered and remained committed to her dream.

In 1991, Pinkett Smith landed her breakthrough role in the television series "A Different World." Her portrayal of Lena James, a college student navigating relationships and personal growth, earned her widespread recognition and praise. The show provided a platform for Pinkett Smith to showcase her talent and establish herself as a rising star in the entertainment industry.

Following her success on "A Different World," Pinkett Smith continued to pursue acting opportunities in both television and film. She appeared in notable projects such as "Menace II Society," "The Nutty Professor," and "Set It Off," further solidifying her reputation as a versatile and talented actress.

In addition to her acting career, Pinkett Smith has also ventured into other areas of the entertainment industry. She formed a band called Wicked Wisdom, showcasing her musical talents and passion for rock music. Pinkett Smith also delved into producing, with projects such as "The Secret Life of Bees" and the popular web series "Red Table Talk," which she hosts alongside her mother and daughter.

Throughout her career, Pinkett Smith has remained dedicated to her craft and committed to using her platform for positive change. She has tackled a wide range of roles, from dramatic performances to action-packed films, consistently showcasing her versatility and talent. Pinkett Smith's commitment to authenticity and her willingness to take on challenging and thought-provoking projects have earned her critical acclaim and a loyal fan base.

In conclusion, Jada Pinkett Smith's education and career beginnings were shaped by her passion for performing, her dedication to honing her craft, and her unwavering determination to succeed. From her early exposure to the arts and her education at the Baltimore School for the Arts to her breakthrough role in "A Different World" and subsequent success in film and other ventures, Pinkett Smith's journey has been marked by resilience, talent, and a strong work ethic. Her continued success in the entertainment industry is a testament to her talent, drive, and the solid foundation provided by her family and upbringing.

CHAPTER 2

PERSONAL LIFE

Relationships And Marriage

P inkett Smith's relationships and marriage have been a topic of public interest and scrutiny throughout her career. She has been open about her personal life, sharing insights and experiences that have resonated with many.

Pinkett Smith's most notable relationship is her marriage to actor Will Smith. The couple met in 1994 when she auditioned for the role of his girlfriend on the popular television series "The Fresh Prince of Bel-Air." Although she did not get the part, their connection was undeniable, and they began dating shortly after.

In 1997, Pinkett Smith and Will Smith tied the knot in a private ceremony. They have since become one of Hollywood's most enduring power couples, known for their chemistry, support of each other's careers, and commitment to their family.

Throughout their marriage, Pinkett Smith and Will Smith have faced their fair share of challenges. They have been open about their struggles, including periods of separation and difficulties in maintaining a strong partnership while navigating the demands of their careers.

One aspect of Pinkett Smith's relationship that has gained attention is her unconventional approach to marriage. She has spoken openly about the concept of "unconventional partnerships" and the importance of personal growth within a committed relationship. Pinkett Smith believes in allowing each partner the freedom to explore their individual passions and desires, while still maintaining a strong bond.

In 2018, Pinkett Smith made headlines when she revealed on her web series "Red Table Talk" that she had an "entanglement" with musician August Alsina during a period of separation from Will Smith. This revelation sparked conversations about open relationships, communication, and the complexities of marriage.

Despite the challenges they have faced, Pinkett Smith and Will Smith have consistently shown a united front and a commitment to working through their issues. They have been vocal about the importance of therapy and open communication in maintaining a healthy relationship.

Another significant aspect of Pinkett Smith's relationships is her strong bond with her children. She has two children with Will Smith, Jaden and Willow, who have both pursued careers in the entertainment industry. Pinkett Smith has been a vocal advocate for supporting her children's individual paths and allowing them to express themselves authentically.

In addition to her marriage and family life, Pinkett Smith has also been open about her friendships and the importance of surrounding herself with a supportive network. She has formed close bonds with fellow actresses such as Queen Latifah and Regina Hall, and regularly expresses gratitude for the friendships that have sustained her throughout her career.

Her/ relationships and marriage have been marked by honesty, resilience, and a commitment to personal growth. She has navigated the challenges of a high-profile marriage while remaining true to herself and her own needs. Pinkett Smith's openness about the complexities of relationships has resonated with many, and she continues to inspire others through her candid discussions on love, marriage, and personal fulfillment.

Relationship with Tupac Shakur

Jada Pinkett Smith's relationship with Tupac Shakur has been a topic of great interest and speculation throughout the years. The deep bond they shared as friends and confidantes has left an indelible mark on both of their lives and continues to be a subject of intrigue and admiration. Let's explore extensively the unique connection between Jada Pinkett Smith and Tupac Shakur.

➢ *The Foundation of Friendship*

Jada Pinkett Smith and Tupac Shakur first met while attending Baltimore School for the Arts in Maryland. The two young, passionate artists quickly formed a strong friendship that endured throughout their lives. They shared a deep understanding, common interests, and a magnetic connection that transcended traditional boundaries.

➢ *Shared Dreams and Artistic Journeys*

They both harbored immense talent and a shared passion for the performing arts. While they pursued separate careers in the entertainment industry, their mutual support and love for one another remained constant. Through their respective pursuits, they constantly inspired and encouraged each other to reach their full artistic potential.

A Bond of Mutual Respect and Empowerment

Jada Pinkett Smith and Tupac Shakur's relationship was characterized by a profound sense of respect and empowerment for one another. They embraced each other's individuality, and their bond was built on a foundation of trust, authenticity, and unconditional support. They navigated both personal and professional challenges together, serving as pillars of strength and inspiration for each other's growth.

➤ *The Influence of Tupac on Jada*

Tupac's impact on Jada Pinkett Smith's life can be seen through her own words and actions. She has often spoken about how Tupac influenced her perspectives on life, art, and society. His unapologetic honesty, artistic brilliance, and commitment to social change left an indelible impression that shaped Jada's outlook on the world.

➤ *A Lasting Connection*

Despite the challenges and tribulations they both faced individually, Jada Pinkett Smith and Tupac Shakur's friendship remained steadfast until Tupac's untimely death in 1996. Jada has continued to honor his memory, paying tribute to him through public statements, social media posts, and by showcasing his lasting impact on her life and career.

➤ *Respecting Privacy and Boundaries*

While Jada Pinkett Smith has shared glimpses into her friendship with Tupac Shakur, she has also emphasized the importance of respecting their privacy and preserving the intimate details of their connection. Understanding the profound and personal nature of their relationship, she has chosen to keep certain aspects private, allowing them to remain as cherished memories within her heart.

In conclusion, Jada Pinkett Smith's relationship with Tupac Shakur was defined by an extraordinary bond that transcended superficial labels. Their friendship was grounded in mutual respect, shared dreams, and unconditional support. Although their time together was tragically cut short, the impact Tupac had on Jada's life is evident in her words and actions. Their unique connection serves as a powerful testament to the enduring impact of true friendship and the transformative power of art and love.

Motherhood and Family Dynamics

Jada's journey as a mother and her family dynamics have been an integral part of her life and career. She has been open and transparent about her experiences, sharing her insights and wisdom with her fans and followers.

Pinkett Smith is a proud mother to two children, Jaden and Willow Smith, whom she shares with her husband, actor Will Smith. She has always prioritized her role as a mother and has been actively involved in their upbringing.

One aspect that sets Pinkett Smith apart as a mother is her commitment to allowing her children to express themselves fully and authentically. She has emphasized the importance of nurturing their individuality and supporting their passions, even if they may deviate from societal norms or expectations.

Pinkett Smith has been vocal about her decision to homeschool her children for a period of time, believing in the importance of providing them with a personalized education that aligns with their interests and values. This approach allowed Jaden and Willow to explore their creativity and pursue their artistic endeavors while also emphasizing the importance of education.

The Smith family dynamic is often characterized by love, support, and open communication. Pinkett Smith has spoken openly about the challenges she has faced as a mother, acknowledging that parenting is not always easy. However, she has emphasized the importance of maintaining a strong bond with her children and fostering an environment where they feel safe to express themselves and share their thoughts and feelings.

Pinkett Smith's own upbringing has played a significant role in shaping her approach to motherhood. She has credited her mother, Adrienne Banfield-Jones, for instilling in her the values of independence, resilience, and self-love. Their close relationship is evident in their joint hosting of the popular web series "Red Table Talk," where they discuss a wide range of topics, including relationships, mental health, and personal growth.

Through "Red Table Talk," Pinkett Smith has created a platform for open and honest conversations, not only with her mother but also with her daughter Willow. The three generations of women come together to share their experiences, perspectives, and insights, creating a space for healing, understanding, and growth. This unique family dynamic has resonated with audiences worldwide, as it showcases the power of vulnerability and the strength that can be found in familial connections.

Pinkett Smith's dedication to her family extends beyond her immediate household. She has spoken about the importance of building a strong community and supporting other mothers. She encourages women to lean on each other for support and guidance, recognizing that motherhood is a journey that is best navigated together.

In conclusion, Jada Pinkett Smith's motherhood and family dynamics have played a significant role in shaping her life and career. Her commitment to allowing her children to express themselves fully, her emphasis on open communication and support, and her dedication to building strong familial connections have made her an inspiring figure for many. Through her transparency and willingness to share her experiences, Pinkett Smith has created a platform for healing, growth, and empowerment, both within her own family and for her fans around the world.

Philanthropy and Activism

Jada Pinkett Smith's philanthropy and activism have been an integral part of her life and career. She has used her platform and influence to bring attention to important social issues and make a positive impact in various areas.

One of the causes that Pinkett Smith is passionate about is mental health. She has been vocal about her own struggles with mental health and has advocated for destigmatizing conversations around it. Through her web series "Red Table Talk," she has provided a safe space for open discussions about mental health, inviting guests to share their stories and experiences. Pinkett Smith's transparency has helped break down barriers and encourage others to seek help and support.

In addition to mental health, Pinkett Smith has been actively involved in advocating for women's rights and empowerment. She has spoken out against gender inequality and has used her platform to highlight the importance of women's voices being heard and respected. Through "Red Table Talk," she has facilitated conversations on topics such as body image, self-worth, and relationships, providing a platform for women to share their experiences and support one another.

Pinkett Smith has also been involved in philanthropic efforts focused on education. She has supported initiatives that provide educational opportunities for underprivileged children, recognizing the transformative power of education in breaking cycles of poverty and creating a better future. Additionally, she has been a strong advocate for homeschooling, believing in the importance of personalized education that caters to each child's unique needs and interests.

Another area of activism that Pinkett Smith has been involved in is environmental conservation. She has expressed concerns about climate change and has encouraged individuals to take action in reducing their carbon footprint. Pinkett Smith has supported organizations that promote sustainable living practices and has spoken about the importance of protecting the planet for future generations.

Furthermore, Pinkett Smith has used her platform to address racial inequality and social justice issues. She has been an advocate for the Black Lives Matter movement, speaking out against systemic racism and police brutality. Pinkett Smith has used her social media platforms to amplify the voices of activists and organizations fighting for racial justice, encouraging her followers to educate themselves and take action.

In addition to her activism, Pinkett Smith has also been involved in various philanthropic endeavors. She has supported organizations such as the Will and Jada Smith Family Foundation, which focuses on providing educational opportunities and empowering underserved communities. Pinkett Smith has also been involved in initiatives that provide clean water access to communities in need.

One of the ways Pinkett Smith demonstrates her commitment to making a positive impact in the world is through her philanthropy and activism. Through her advocacy for mental health, women's rights, education, environmental conservation, racial equality, and various philanthropic efforts, she has used her platform to raise awareness, inspire change, and support those in need. Pinkett Smith's dedication to social issues and her willingness to use her voice for good have made her an influential figure in the realm of philanthropy and activism.

JADA PINKETT SMITH BIO

CHAPTER 3

ACTING CAREER

Breakthrough Role in "A Different World"

Her breakthrough role in "A Different World" was a significant milestone in her career and a defining moment for her as an actress. The popular television series, which aired from 1987 to 1993, was a spin-off of "The Cosby Show" and focused on the experiences of students at the fictional historically black college, Hillman College.

Pinkett Smith joined the cast in the show's second season, playing the character of Lena James, a young and ambitious student with a strong passion for the arts. Her portrayal of Lena showcased her talent as an actress and allowed her to shine in a role that resonated with many viewers.

Lena James quickly became a fan-favorite character due to her relatable qualities and the depth that Pinkett Smith brought to the role. Lena was depicted as a confident and independent young woman who faced various challenges and triumphs throughout her college journey. Pinkett Smith's performance captured the complexities of Lena's character, showcasing her vulnerability, resilience, and determination.

One of the most notable storylines involving Lena James was her struggle with an unplanned pregnancy. This storyline tackled important issues surrounding reproductive rights, decision-making, and the support systems available to young women in similar situations. Pinkett Smith's portrayal of Lena's emotional journey was praised for its authenticity and sensitivity, highlighting her ability to tackle complex and relevant topics with grace.

Beyond her character's personal storyline, Pinkett Smith's presence on "A Different World" contributed to the show's overall impact in addressing social issues. The series tackled topics such as racism, sexism, HIV/AIDS awareness, and activism, providing a platform for important discussions within the context of higher education. Pinkett Smith's involvement in these storylines helped bring attention to these issues and sparked conversations among viewers.

"A Different World" also provided Pinkett Smith with an opportunity to showcase her talent as a singer. She performed several musical numbers throughout the series, further highlighting her versatility as an entertainer.

Pinkett Smith's role in "A Different World" not only launched her career but also solidified her as a talented actress with a strong social consciousness. The show's portrayal of college life and its exploration of social issues resonated with audiences, and Pinkett Smith's performance as Lena James contributed to the show's success.

Her time on "A Different World" laid the foundation for Pinkett Smith's future endeavors in both acting and activism. It showcased her ability to tackle complex characters and storylines while also addressing important social issues. The show served as a platform for Pinkett Smith to use her voice and influence to bring attention to topics that were often overlooked or marginalized.

Pinkett Smith's breakthrough role in "A Different World" was a pivotal moment in her career. It allowed her to showcase her talent as an actress, tackle important social issues, and establish herself as an influential figure in the entertainment industry. Her portrayal of Lena James remains a memorable and impactful part of television history.

Film Debut and Rising Stardom

Jada Pinkett Smith's film debut and rising stardom can be traced back to her breakthrough role in the 1993 film "Menace II Society." Directed by Allen and Albert Hughes, the crime drama explored the harsh realities of life in South Central Los Angeles. Pinkett Smith portrayed Ronnie, a single mother who becomes involved with a young man caught up in a life of crime.

Pinkett Smith's performance in "Menace II Society" was widely praised by critics and audiences alike. Her portrayal of Ronnie showcased her ability to bring depth and authenticity to her characters, capturing the struggles and complexities of a woman trying to navigate a dangerous environment while protecting her child. Her performance was both vulnerable and powerful, leaving a lasting impact on viewers.

Following the success of "Menace II Society," Pinkett Smith continued to make waves in the film industry with her roles in movies such as "Jason's Lyric" (1994) and "Set It Off" (1996). In "Jason's Lyric," she played the love interest of the titular character, portraying a woman trapped in an abusive relationship. Pinkett Smith's performance garnered critical acclaim, further solidifying her talent as an actress.

However, it was her role as Stony in "Set It Off" that truly propelled Pinkett Smith into the spotlight. The crime thriller, directed by F. Gary Gray, followed four friends who turn to bank robbery as a means to escape their dire circumstances. Pinkett Smith's portrayal of Stony, a determined and courageous woman seeking justice, showcased her range as an actress and earned her widespread recognition.

"Set It Off" became a cultural phenomenon, resonating with audiences for its exploration of female empowerment, friendship, and socio-economic struggles. Pinkett Smith's performance was particularly praised for its emotional depth and the way she brought humanity and complexity to Stony's character. The film solidified Pinkett Smith's status as a rising star in Hollywood and opened doors for her to take on even more diverse and challenging roles.

In the years that followed, Pinkett Smith continued to showcase her versatility as an actress through roles in films such as "The Nutty Professor" (1996), "Ali" (2001), and "Collateral" (2004). She also ventured into producing, co-producing the critically acclaimed film "The Secret Life of Bees" (2008) and the popular TV series "Hawthorne" (2009-2011).

Pinkett Smith's rising stardom was not limited to the big screen. She also made notable appearances on television, including her role as Fish Mooney in the hit series "Gotham" (2014-2019) and her hosting duties on the talk show "Red Table Talk" (2018-present), where she engages in candid conversations with her family and guests about various topics.

Throughout her career, Pinkett Smith has consistently demonstrated her talent, versatility, and commitment to telling stories that resonate with audiences. Her performances have garnered critical acclaim and earned her numerous accolades, including nominations for prestigious awards such as the NAACP Image Awards and the MTV Movie Awards.

Beyond her success as an actress, Pinkett Smith has also become known for her advocacy work and philanthropy. She uses her platform to raise awareness about important social issues, particularly those affecting women, children, and marginalized communities. Pinkett Smith's dedication to activism further solidifies her status as an influential figure in both the entertainment industry and society as a whole.

Jada Pinkett Smith's film debut and rising stardom have been marked by exceptional performances, diverse roles, and a commitment to using her platform for positive change. From her breakthrough role in "Menace II Society" to her powerful portrayal in "Set It Off" and her continued success in both film and television, Pinkett Smith has proven herself to be a talented and influential force in the entertainment industry. Her impact reaches far beyond her acting abilities, as she continues to inspire and empower others through her advocacy work and philanthropy.

Collaboration with Will Smith and Success in Blockbusters

Jada Pinkett Smith's collaboration with her husband, Will Smith, has been a significant factor in her success in blockbuster films. The couple has worked together on multiple projects, showcasing their chemistry and talent as a dynamic duo onscreen.

One of their earliest collaborations was in the 1995 action-comedy film "Bad Boys," directed by Michael Bay. In the film, Will Smith plays Detective Mike Lowrey, while Jada Pinkett Smith portrays his love interest, Lisa. Their onscreen chemistry was palpable, and their performances brought humor and depth to their respective characters. "Bad Boys" was a commercial success, further establishing Will Smith as a leading actor and introducing Jada Pinkett Smith to a wider audience.

The success of "Bad Boys" led to its sequel, "Bad Boys II," released in 2003. Once again, Will Smith and Jada Pinkett Smith reprised their roles as Mike and Lisa, respectively. The film was another box office hit, solidifying their status as a power couple in Hollywood.

In 2001, Jada Pinkett Smith joined the cast of the science fiction film "The Matrix Reloaded" and its sequel "The Matrix Revolutions" (both released in 2003). While Will Smith did not appear in these films, his influence was still felt as he had been originally considered for the role of Neo, which eventually went to Keanu Reeves. Jada Pinkett Smith played the character Niobe, a skilled pilot and resistance leader. Her performance showcased her versatility as an actress and added another successful franchise to her resume.

Another notable collaboration between Jada Pinkett Smith and Will Smith was in the 2008 superhero film "Hancock." Directed by Peter Berg, the film starred Will Smith as the titular character, a reluctant superhero with personal issues. Jada Pinkett Smith portrayed Mary, the wife of Hancock's best friend. Their onscreen chemistry and emotional performances added depth to the film, which went on to become a box office success.

One of the most significant collaborations between Jada Pinkett Smith and Will Smith was in the 2001 biographical sports drama film "Ali," directed by Michael Mann. Will Smith portrayed the legendary boxer Muhammad Ali, while Jada Pinkett Smith played his first wife, Sonji Roi. Their performances were critically acclaimed, with Jada Pinkett Smith capturing the spirit and strength of Sonji Roi. The film received several accolades, including Academy Award nominations, further solidifying their status as talented actors.

In addition to their collaborations in blockbuster films, Jada Pinkett Smith and Will Smith have also worked together as producers.

They co-produced the 2001 biographical drama film "Kingdom Come," which starred an ensemble cast including Jada Pinkett Smith herself. Their production company, Overbrook Entertainment, has been involved in various successful projects, showcasing their ability to bring compelling stories to the screen.

Jada Pinkett Smith's collaboration with her husband has been instrumental in her success in blockbuster films. Their onscreen chemistry and talent as actors have resulted in memorable performances and box office hits. Their collaborations have showcased their versatility as individuals and as a couple, further establishing them as influential figures in the entertainment industry.

Notable Filmography and Awards

Jada Pinkett Smith has had a notable filmography throughout her career, with roles in a variety of genres and critically acclaimed performances. Here are some of her notable films and awards:

i. ***"Set It Off" (1996)***: In this crime thriller, Jada Pinkett Smith played the role of Stony, one of four women who turn to bank robbery to escape their difficult lives. Her performance was highly praised, earning her an NAACP Image Award nomination for Outstanding Actress in a Motion Picture.

ii. ***"The Nutty Professor" (1996)***: Jada Pinkett Smith portrayed Carla Purty, the love interest of Eddie Murphy's character, in this comedy film. Her performance showcased her comedic timing and charm.

iii.   ***"Collateral" (2004)***: In this thriller directed by Michael Mann, Jada Pinkett Smith played the role of Annie Farrell, a prosecutor who becomes involved with a hitman played by Tom Cruise. Her performance earned her critical acclaim and an NAACP Image Award nomination for Outstanding Supporting Actress in a Motion Picture.

iv.   ***"The Women" (2008)***: Jada Pinkett Smith joined an ensemble cast including Meg Ryan and Annette Bening in this comedy-drama film. She portrayed Alex Fisher, a lesbian author, and her performance added depth to the film's exploration of female relationships.

v.   ***"Girls Trip" (2017)***: Jada Pinkett Smith starred alongside Regina Hall, Queen Latifah, and Tiffany Haddish in this comedy film about a group of friends who reunite for a wild weekend in New Orleans. Her performance as Lisa Cooper, a reserved and cautious woman, was widely praised for its comedic timing and vulnerability. She received an NAACP Image Award nomination for Outstanding Supporting Actress in a Motion Picture.

In addition to her notable film roles, Jada Pinkett Smith has also received recognition for her work on television. She has been a part of the cast of the popular TV series "Gotham" since 2014, playing the character Fish Mooney. Her portrayal of the complex and ruthless crime boss has garnered critical acclaim.

Throughout her career, Jada Pinkett Smith has received several awards and nominations for her performances. She has won multiple NAACP Image Awards, including Outstanding Actress in a Motion Picture for "The Nutty Professor" and Outstanding Supporting Actress in a Motion Picture for "Collateral." She has also been honored with the BET Honors Award for Excellence in Entertainment and the Black Reel Award for Best Supporting Actress for her role in "Collateral."

In addition to her individual accolades, Jada Pinkett Smith has received recognition for her contributions as a producer. She was nominated for a Primetime Emmy Award as an executive producer of the talk show "Red Table Talk," which she hosts alongside her daughter, Willow Smith, and her mother, Adrienne Banfield-Norris.

Jada Pinkett Smith's filmography is filled with diverse roles that showcase her talent and versatility as an actress. Her performances have garnered critical acclaim and numerous awards, further solidifying her status as a respected figure in the entertainment industry.

CHAPTER 4

MUSIC CAREER

Band Wicked Wisdom

Pinkett Smith's formation of the band Wicked Wisdom marked a significant milestone in her career as an artist. The band was formed in 2002, with Jada serving as the lead vocalist. Wicked Wisdom is a heavy metal band that incorporates elements of rock, alternative, and nu-metal into their sound.

Her decision to form Wicked Wisdom was a departure from her previous work in acting and showcased her versatility as an artist. She had always been passionate about music, and forming a band allowed her to explore a different creative outlet and express herself in a new way.

The formation of Wicked Wisdom was not without its challenges. As an African-American woman fronting a heavy metal band, Jada faced criticism and skepticism from some within the music industry and fanbase. However, she remained undeterred and used this opportunity to break down barriers and challenge stereotypes.

Wicked Wisdom gained attention through their energetic live performances and powerful music. Their sound was characterized by heavy guitar riffs, intense drumming, and Jada's dynamic vocals. Their lyrics often touched on themes of empowerment, self-expression, and personal growth.

In 2004, Wicked Wisdom released their self-titled debut album, which received mixed reviews from critics. However, the band's live performances garnered praise for their high energy and stage

31

presence. They went on to tour with notable rock acts such as Sevendust and Britney Spears.

Despite the initial skepticism surrounding Jada's involvement in a heavy metal band, Wicked Wisdom gradually gained recognition and respect within the music industry. Their dedication to their craft and commitment to delivering powerful performances resonated with audiences.

Jada's involvement in Wicked Wisdom also allowed her to connect with fans on a deeper level. Through her music, she shared personal stories and experiences, including her struggles with mental health and the importance of self-empowerment. This vulnerability and authenticity further endeared her to audiences and solidified her status as a relatable and inspiring figure.

While Wicked Wisdom's activity has been sporadic in recent years, Jada's involvement in the band remains an important part of her artistic journey. The formation of Wicked Wisdom showcased her fearlessness in pursuing her passions and breaking down barriers within the music industry.

The formation of the band Wicked Wisdom demonstrated her willingness to explore new artistic avenues and challenge expectations. Through their music, Wicked Wisdom provided a platform for Jada to express herself authentically and connect with audiences on a deeper level. This chapter in her career further solidified her status as a multi-talented artist and exemplified her commitment to pushing boundaries and defying stereotypes.

Musical Style

Jada Pinkett Smith's musical style and influences can be described as a blend of various genres, including heavy metal, rock, alternative, and nu-metal. Her musical journey with Wicked Wisdom showcased her versatility as an artist and her willingness to explore different creative outlets.

In terms of musical style, Jada's involvement in Wicked Wisdom allowed her to delve into the world of heavy metal, a genre known for its aggressive guitar riffs, intense drumming, and powerful vocals. Her dynamic and energetic stage presence complemented the band's sound, creating a captivating live performance experience.

While Jada's musical style was heavily influenced by the heavy metal genre, she also incorporated elements of rock, alternative, and nu-metal into Wicked Wisdom's sound. These influences can be heard in the band's use of distorted guitar tones, catchy hooks, and melodic choruses. This blending of genres helped to create a unique and distinctive sound for Wicked Wisdom.

In terms of influences, Jada has cited various artists and bands that have inspired her musical journey. She has mentioned iconic rock bands such as Guns N' Roses, Metallica, and AC/DC as influences on her music. These bands are known for their high-energy performances, powerful vocals, and memorable guitar riffs, which align with the elements present in Wicked Wisdom's music.

Additionally, Jada has spoken about how artists like Korn and Limp Bizkit influenced her musical style. These nu-metal bands were known for their fusion of heavy metal, hip-hop, and alternative rock, creating a unique sound that resonated with Jada and influenced the direction of Wicked Wisdom's music.

Jada's musical style and influences also reflect her personal experiences and emotions. Through her lyrics and performances, she has shared stories of empowerment, self-expression, and personal growth. These themes are often present in heavy metal and rock music, as these genres have a history of addressing societal issues and personal struggles.

Her musical style can be characterized as a fusion of heavy metal, rock, alternative, and nu-metal. Her willingness to explore different genres and incorporate various influences into her music showcases her versatility as an artist. Through Wicked Wisdom, Jada was able to express herself authentically and connect with audiences on a deeper level, solidifying her status as a multi-talented artist in the music industry.

Touring and Live Performances

Her touring and live performances have been a significant aspect of her musical career. With her band Wicked Wisdom, she has captivated audiences with her dynamic stage presence, powerful vocals, and energetic performances.

During their touring years, Wicked Wisdom performed at various music festivals and venues, sharing their unique blend of heavy metal, rock, alternative, and nu-metal with fans around the world. Jada's ability to command the stage and engage the audience created an electrifying atmosphere that left a lasting impression on concert-goers.

One notable aspect of Jada's live performances is her commitment to delivering an authentic and passionate performance. She pours her heart and soul into every song, connecting with the audience on an emotional level. Jada's lyrics often touch on personal experiences, empowerment, and self-expression, allowing fans to resonate with her music and feel a sense of unity during her live shows.

Another highlight of Jada's live performances is her incredible vocal range and control. She effortlessly transitions between powerful, soulful vocals and aggressive screams, showcasing her versatility as a vocalist. This vocal prowess adds depth and intensity to Wicked Wisdom's music, creating a captivating live experience for fans.

In addition to her vocals, Jada's stage presence is also a key element of her live performances. She exudes confidence and charisma, commanding attention from the moment she steps on stage. Her energetic movements, engaging interactions with the crowd, and captivating stage persona create an immersive and unforgettable concert experience.

Furthermore, Jada's touring with Wicked Wisdom allowed her to showcase her versatility as an artist. While she is primarily known as an actress, her musical talents shine through during live performances. This ability to excel in different creative outlets demonstrates her dedication to exploring her artistic passions and pushing boundaries.

Throughout her touring years, Jada Pinkett Smith's live performances garnered critical acclaim and earned her a devoted fan base. Her ability to seamlessly blend genres, deliver powerful vocals, and connect with the audience has solidified her reputation as a captivating live performer.

So, Jada Pinkett Smith's touring and live performances with Wicked Wisdom have been characterized by her dynamic stage presence, powerful vocals, and ability to connect with the audience. Her commitment to authenticity, versatility as an artist, and engaging performances have made her a standout figure in the music industry. Whether performing at music festivals or intimate venues, Jada's live shows leave a lasting impact on fans, showcasing her talent and passion for music.

CHAPTER 5

Overbrook Entertainment

Jada Pinkett Smith co-founded Overbrook Entertainment, a production company, with her husband Will Smith and business partner James Lassiter in 1997. The company was named after the neighborhood in West Philadelphia where Will Smith was born and raised.

Overbrook Entertainment has been involved in the production of numerous successful films and television shows. One of their earliest projects was the hit sitcom "All of Us," which aired from 2003 to 2007. The show, which was loosely based on the blended family of Will Smith and Jada Pinkett Smith, received critical acclaim and was praised for its realistic portrayal of modern family dynamics.

Overbrook Entertainment has also produced several blockbuster films, including "Hitch" (2005), "The Pursuit of Happyness" (2006), and "I Am Legend" (2007). These films starred Will Smith and were not only commercial successes but also received positive reviews from critics.

In addition to working with her husband, Jada Pinkett Smith has also produced projects independently through Overbrook Entertainment. One notable example is the biographical drama film "The Karate Kid" (2010), which starred Jaden Smith, their son, in the lead role. The film was a remake of the 1984 classic.

Overbrook Entertainment has also ventured into the world of animation with films like "Annie" (2014), a modern retelling of the beloved musical. The film starred Quvenzhané Wallis as Annie and featured an ensemble cast that included Jamie Foxx, Rose Byrne, and Cameron Diaz.

Production Company Projects and Successes

Overbrook Entertainment has had a string of successful projects throughout its existence. One of their earliest successes was the hit sitcom "All of Us," which aired from 2003 to 2007. The show, loosely based on the blended family of Jada Pinkett Smith and Will Smith, received critical acclaim for its realistic portrayal of modern family dynamics.

In the film industry, Overbrook Entertainment has produced several blockbuster hits. One of their notable successes was "Hitch" (2005), a romantic comedy starring Will Smith as a professional dating consultant. The film was a commercial success, grossing over $368 million worldwide. It showcased Overbrook Entertainment's ability to produce crowd-pleasing films with broad appeal.

Another significant success for Overbrook Entertainment was "The Pursuit of Happyness" (2006), a biographical drama based on the life of entrepreneur Chris Gardner. The film starred Will Smith in the lead role and was not only a box office hit, grossing over $307 million worldwide, but also received critical acclaim. Will Smith's performance earned him an Academy Award nomination for Best Actor, further solidifying Overbrook Entertainment's reputation for producing high-quality films.

In 2007, Overbrook Entertainment continued its winning streak with "I Am Legend," a post-apocalyptic action thriller also starring Will Smith. The film grossed over $585 million worldwide and received positive reviews from critics. It showcased the company's ability to produce visually stunning and commercially successful films.

Overbrook Entertainment also ventured into producing projects independently from Will Smith. One notable example is the famous movie, "The Karate Kid" (2010), a biographical drama film starring Jaden Smith, the son of Jada Pinkett Smith and Will Smith. was a box office success, grossing over $350 million worldwide. It showcased Overbrook Entertainment's ability to nurture and promote emerging talent within the industry.

Overbrook Entertainment has also exploration of the world of animation with films like "Annie" (2014) highlights the company's versatility in producing different genres of films. While the film received mixed reviews from critics, it still managed to be a financial success.

In recent years, Overbrook Entertainment has expanded its focus to include television series and digital content. They have been involved in the production of shows like "The Queen Latifah Show" and "The Get Down," a musical drama series created by Baz Luhrmann for Netflix. These ventures demonstrate Overbrook Entertainment's adaptability and willingness to explore new platforms and mediums.

Overbrook Entertainment has had a significant impact on Jada Pinkett Smith's career as a producer. The company has produced a diverse range of projects, from sitcoms to blockbuster films to television series. Through Overbrook Entertainment, Jada Pinkett Smith has been able to contribute to the entertainment industry both in front of and behind the camera, showcasing her multifaceted talent as a producer.

Fashion and Beauty Ventures

In addition to her successful career in the entertainment industry, Pinkett Smith has also made a name for herself in the world of fashion and beauty. Known for her impeccable sense of style and stunning red carpet looks, she has ventured into various fashion and beauty ventures that have further solidified her status as a fashion icon.

Jada Pinkett Smith has collaborated with renowned fashion designers and brands to create her own fashion lines. One notable collaboration was with designer Alberta Ferretti, resulting in the creation of the "Alberta Ferretti Limited Edition by Jada Pinkett Smith" collection. The collection showcased Jada's personal style, featuring feminine and elegant designs that reflected her sophisticated taste. The line included a range of evening gowns, cocktail dresses, and separates that catered to women who desired timeless and glamorous pieces.

In addition to her collaboration with Alberta Ferretti, Jada Pinkett Smith has also partnered with other fashion brands. She has been an ambassador for luxury fashion house Gucci, representing the brand at various events and showcasing their designs on the red carpet. Her association with Gucci has further cemented her status as a fashion influencer and style icon.

She has also ventured into the beauty industry, launching her own line of beauty products. She founded the beauty brand "Hey Humans" in 2020, which focuses on sustainable and eco-friendly personal care products. The brand offers a range of products, including body washes, lotions, deodorants, and toothpaste, all made with clean and natural ingredients. Jada's commitment to sustainability and environmental consciousness is reflected in the brand's packaging, which is made from recycled materials.

Furthermore, Jada Pinkett Smith has been vocal about promoting self-care and embracing natural beauty. She has shared her skincare and wellness routines with her followers, emphasizing the importance of taking care of oneself both physically and mentally. Her transparency and authenticity in discussing her own beauty journey have resonated with many, inspiring others to embrace their natural beauty and prioritize self-care.

Jada Pinkett Smith's fashion and beauty ventures have not only showcased her impeccable sense of style and beauty, but they have also provided platforms for her to promote inclusivity and diversity. She has been an advocate for representation in the fashion and beauty industries, using her influence to push for more diversity in campaigns and runway shows. Through her collaborations and brand partnerships, she has helped to create more opportunities for underrepresented voices in the industry.

In all, Jada Pinkett Smith's fashion and beauty ventures have allowed her to express her creativity and passion for style. Her collaborations with renowned designers, her own beauty brand, and her advocacy for inclusivity have solidified her status as a fashion icon and influential figure in the fashion and beauty industries. Jada's impact extends beyond her on-screen talent, as she continues to inspire and empower others through her fashion and beauty endeavors.

Advocacy for Mental Health and Wellness

Jada has been a vocal advocate for mental health and wellness, using her platform to raise awareness and promote self-care practices. She has openly shared her own experiences with mental health challenges, emphasizing the importance of prioritizing mental well-being and seeking help when needed.

One of the ways Jada Pinkett Smith has advocated for mental health is through her talk show, Red Table Talk. The show, co-hosted by Jada, her daughter Willow Smith, and her mother Adrienne Banfield-Norris, tackles various topics including mental health, addiction, and trauma. Through candid and honest conversations, Jada and her co-hosts create a safe space for guests to share their personal stories and struggles, aiming to reduce stigma and provide support to viewers who may be going through similar experiences.

Jada has also used social media as a platform to discuss mental health and wellness. She regularly shares inspirational quotes, personal reflections, and self-care tips with her followers. By sharing her own journey and encouraging open dialogue, she aims to foster a sense of community and encourage individuals to prioritize their mental well-being.

In addition to her advocacy work, Jada Pinkett Smith has also been involved in various initiatives that promote mental health and wellness. She has been a supporter of organizations such as the Mental Health Foundation and the Jed Foundation, which focus on raising awareness and providing resources for mental health issues. Through her involvement, she helps to amplify the voices of these organizations and contribute to the ongoing conversation surrounding mental health.

Furthermore, Jada Pinkett Smith has emphasized the importance of self-care practices in maintaining good mental health. She encourages individuals to engage in activities that bring them joy and provide a sense of peace, whether it be through exercise, meditation, or creative outlets. By sharing her own self-care routines and promoting these practices, she aims to inspire others to prioritize their mental well-being and find healthy coping mechanisms.

Jada Pinkett Smith's advocacy for mental health and wellness extends beyond her public platform. She actively engages in self-reflection and personal growth, seeking therapy and counseling to navigate her own mental health journey. By openly discussing her own experiences with therapy, she helps to break down the stigma surrounding seeking professional help and encourages others to do the same.

Jada Pinkett Smith's advocacy for mental health and wellness is a testament to her commitment to creating a more compassionate and understanding society. Through her talk show, social media presence, and involvement in various initiatives, she uses her platform to raise awareness, reduce stigma, and provide support for individuals struggling with mental health challenges. Her vulnerability, authenticity, and dedication to promoting mental well-being make her a powerful advocate and role model in the field of mental health advocacy.

JADA PINKETT SMITH BIO

CHAPTER 6

PHILANTHROPY AND SOCIAL ACTIVISM

Involvement in Humanitarian Causes

The talented actress, producer, and philanthropist, has significantly contributed to various humanitarian causes throughout her career. She has consistently used her platform and resources to advocate for social change, promote equality, and raise awareness about critical issues affecting marginalized communities. Let's explore some of the notable areas of Jada Pinkett Smith's involvement in humanitarian causes.

> *Women's Empowerment*: Pinkett Smith has been a vocal advocate for women's rights and empowerment. She has spoken out against gender-based violence, advocated for equal pay, and highlighted the importance of women's representation in various industries. Through her various media platforms and engagement in organizations like the Women's Global Empowerment Fund, she has worked to empower women and create a more inclusive society.

> *Mental Health Awareness*: The issue of mental health holds personal significance for Pinkett Smith. She has been transparent about her own struggles and has used her platform to spark conversations around mental health. Through her talk show, "Red Table Talk," she has hosted discussions on topics such as addiction, depression, and trauma, aiming to reduce the stigma surrounding mental health and provide support for those in need.

> *Youth Empowerment and Education*: Pinkett Smith recognizes the importance of education and its role in empowering young individuals. She has been involved in

initiatives focused on providing educational opportunities and resources to children and underserved communities. Her involvement in organizations like the Will and Jada Smith Family Foundation evidences her commitment to nurturing young talent and fostering academic excellence.

> ***Human Trafficking and Exploitation***: She is a passionate advocate against human trafficking and the exploitation of vulnerable populations. She has supported organizations such as Polaris and the Rock Against Trafficking Foundation. Through her involvement, she has worked towards raising awareness, providing support for survivors, and campaigning for legislation aimed at combating human trafficking.

> ***Racial Justice and Equity***: As an African-American woman, Pinkett Smith has been actively engaged in discussions about racial justice and equity. She has used her platform to amplify voices of marginalized communities and has advocated for systemic change. Her commitment to addressing racial disparities is exemplified by her involvement with organizations like Black Girls Rock! and her outspoken support for the Black Lives Matter movement.

Beyond these specific causes, Pinkett Smith has demonstrated a broader commitment to social activism and inspiring positive change. She encourages empathy and compassion through her online platforms, engaging with her followers on a range of societal issues. Her multifaceted dedication to humanitarian causes showcases her desire to create a more equitable and inclusive world.

In summary, Jada Pinkett Smith's involvement in humanitarian causes spans a wide range of issues, from women's empowerment and mental health awareness to youth education, human trafficking, and racial justice. Her commitment to making a difference, using her platform, and supporting organizations working towards social progress shines a light on the potential for celebrities to effect meaningful change in society.

Advocacy for Women's Rights and Empowerment

Jada Pinkett Smith has been a passionate advocate for women's rights and empowerment throughout her career. She has used her platform as an actress, producer, and philanthropist to raise awareness about gender inequalities, advocate for equal opportunities, and empower women to embrace their voices and potential. Let's delve into some aspects of Jada Pinkett Smith's advocacy for women's rights and empowerment.

> ➤ *Speaking Out Against Gender-Based Violence*: Pinkett Smith has been vocal about pressing issues such as domestic violence and sexual assault. She has used her influential platform to lend a voice to survivors and raise awareness about the prevalence of these forms of gender-based violence. Her support for organizations like the Domestic Violence Intervention Program reflects her commitment to providing resources and support for victims and survivors.

> ➤ *Equal Pay and Gender Equality*: Pinkett Smith is a staunch advocate for gender equality in the workplace. She has spoken publicly about the persistent wage gap and the need for equal pay for equal work. Through her activism, she aims to challenge systemic barriers that prevent women from achieving financial parity and equal opportunities in their careers.

47

> ***Representation and Diversity***: She has been an advocate for diverse representation in the media and entertainment industry. She has highlighted the importance of diverse storytelling and the need for increased opportunities for women of all backgrounds in film, television, and other creative industries. Her production company, Westbrook Studios, actively promotes inclusion and provides platforms for underrepresented voices.

> ***Empowering Young Women***: Pinkett Smith is deeply committed to empowering young women and instilling in them a sense of self-worth. She has engaged in discussions about self-esteem, body positivity, and the pressures faced by young women in today's society. Through her work on platforms like "Red Table Talk," she addresses issues that impact the lives of young women while offering guidance and support.

> ***Mentorship and Collaboration***: She recognizes the importance of mentorship and collaboration among women. She encourages women to support and uplift each other, fostering an environment of solidarity and empowerment. Her open and inclusive approach creates spaces for women to share their experiences and learn from one another.

Her advocacy for women's rights and empowerment extends beyond her public voice. She has actively engaged in philanthropic endeavors, supporting organizations promoting women's education, leadership development, and economic empowerment. Her involvement with organizations like Girls Inc. and the Women's Global Empowerment Fund demonstrates her commitment to creating opportunities for women from all backgrounds to thrive.

Jada Pinkett Smith's advocacy for women's rights and empowerment is both impactful and meaningful. Through her platform, she amplifies the voices of women, raises awareness about gender inequalities, and promotes inclusive opportunities for women in various sectors. Her commitment to empowering young women and fostering an environment of support emphasizes the importance of collective action in achieving gender equality.

Support for Education and Youth Development

Pinkett Smith has been a strong advocate for education and youth development throughout her career. She recognizes the transformative power of education and the importance of providing opportunities for young individuals to reach their full potential. Through her philanthropic efforts and personal involvement, she has made significant contributions to improving educational access, promoting academic excellence, and empowering young people. Here are some aspects where Jada Pinkett Smith's supports education and youth development.

➤ *Educational Access*: She has been actively involved in initiatives that aim to increase educational access for underserved communities. She understands the importance of breaking down barriers that hinder disadvantaged young people from accessing quality education. Through her engagement with organizations like the Will and Jada Smith Family Foundation, she has worked to provide educational resources, scholarships, and mentorship programs to support students in need.

➤ *STEM Education*: Pinkett Smith recognizes the value of science, technology, engineering, and mathematics (STEM) education in preparing young people for the future. She has advocated for increased focus on STEM programs in schools and has supported organizations and initiatives that promote STEM learning opportunities for youth. By championing STEM education, Pinkett Smith helps young individuals develop essential skills and fosters their interest in fields that are critical for the advancement of society.

➢ *Financial Literacy and Entrepreneurship*: Pinkett Smith emphasizes the importance of financial literacy and entrepreneurship as essential components of youth development. She has encouraged young people to develop financial skills, cultivate an entrepreneurial mindset, and explore opportunities for economic empowerment. Her support for programs that offer financial education and entrepreneurship training demonstrates her commitment to equipping young individuals with the tools necessary for financial independence and success.

➢ *Mental Health and Emotional Well-being*: Jada understands the significance of addressing mental health and emotional well-being among young people. Through her talk show, "Red Table Talk," she has facilitated discussions on topics such as self-esteem, mental health challenges, and resilience. By openly sharing her own experiences and providing a platform for honest conversations, she aims to promote mental wellness and emotional growth among youth.

➢ *Youth Mentorship*: She is an advocate for mentorship and recognizes the positive impact of having strong role models in young people's lives. Through her involvement in mentorship programs and partnerships with various organizations, she has helped create opportunities for young individuals to receive guidance, support, and inspiration from mentors who can help shape their futures.

In addition to her involvement in specific programs, Pinkett Smith uses her celebrity status and media platforms to raise awareness and promote the importance of education and youth development. She encourages young people to embrace their passions, set ambitious goals, and persistently pursue their dreams. Her commitment to education and youth empowerment exemplifies her dedication to investing in the next generation.

Jada Pinkett Smith's support for education and youth development is grounded in her belief in the power of education and the potential of young individuals. Through her philanthropic endeavors, personal engagement, and public advocacy, she actively promotes educational access, STEM education, financial literacy, mental health, mentorship, and overall empowerment of young people. Her efforts serve as a guiding light towards a more equitable and promising future for the youth.

Initiatives in Environmental Conservation

The accomplished actress and philanthropist, is dedicated to environmental conservation and sustainability. She has actively supported initiatives aimed at protecting the environment, raising awareness about climate change, and promoting sustainable practices. Let's explore some of the notable aspects of Jada Pinkett Smith's initiatives in environmental conservation.

> *Plastic Pollution Awareness*: Pinkett Smith has been vocal about the issue of plastic pollution and its devastating impact on marine ecosystems. She has used her platform to raise awareness about the importance of reducing single-use plastic consumption and promoting sustainable alternatives. Through her participation in campaigns like Plastic Free July, she has encouraged individuals to make conscious choices to minimize plastic waste.

➤ **Wildlife Conservation**: She has demonstrated her commitment to wildlife conservation by advocating for the protection of endangered species. She has supported organizations like Oceana, which focuses on preserving the world's oceans and marine life. Her involvement in efforts to protect wildlife habitats and raise awareness about the importance of biodiversity shows her dedication to safeguarding the natural world.

➤ **Climate Change** Awareness: Pinkett Smith has been active in highlighting the urgent need to address climate change. Her engagement in initiatives like Earth Day and her social media presence have been instrumental in spreading awareness about the impact of climate change and the importance of sustainable actions to mitigate its effects. By sharing information and promoting sustainable practices, she encourages individuals to take action and be mindful of their environmental footprint.

➤ **Environmental Education**: Pinkett Smith recognizes the significance of environmental education in nurturing a more sustainable future. She supports programs and initiatives that offer educational resources to young people, emphasizing the importance of eco-consciousness and environmental stewardship. By empowering youth with knowledge and inspiring them to take an active role in conservation, she contributes to building a generation of environmentally conscious individuals.

➤ **Renewable Energy**: She has expressed support for renewable energy sources as part of the solution to combat climate change. She has highlighted the benefits of renewable energy alternatives like solar power and has encouraged the adoption of sustainable energy practices to reduce reliance on fossil fuels and minimize carbon emissions. Her promotion of clean and renewable energy sources aligns with her commitment to a more sustainable future.

Beyond specific initiatives, Pinkett Smith leads by example through her own lifestyle choices. She incorporates sustainable practices into her daily life, such as recycling, using eco-friendly products, and making conscious decisions to minimize her environmental impact. By living out her environmental values, she inspires others to follow suit.

Jada Pinkett Smith's initiatives in environmental conservation reflect her commitment to fostering a sustainable future. Through her advocacy, awareness-raising efforts, support for organizations, and personal lifestyle choices, she demonstrates a firm dedication to the protection of the environment, wildlife conservation, and addressing pressing issues like plastic pollution and climate change. Her efforts inspire individuals to contribute to the collective responsibility of caring for our planet.

JADA PINKETT SMITH BIO

CHAPTER 7

CONTROVERSIES AND CHALLENGES

Public Scrutiny of Personal Life

Just like many public figures, has experienced her fair share of public scrutiny concerning her personal life. As a prominent actress and public figure, her personal relationships, family dynamics, and personal choices have often been under intense scrutiny and public speculation. Living in the public eye can be challenging, and Pinkett Smith has faced her share of criticism, judgment, and invasive questioning.

One such example of public scrutiny regarding Pinkett Smith's personal life is her marriage to actor Will Smith. Throughout their relationship, there have been numerous rumors and tabloid stories speculating about their marriage, alleged infidelities, and claims of an open marriage. Pinkett Smith and Smith have chosen to address these rumors and provide insights into their relationship through their Facebook Watch show, "Red Table Talk." The show provides a platform for open and honest conversations about various topics, including their own experiences as a couple.

In addressing the public scrutiny, Pinkett Smith has displayed remarkable resilience and transparency. She has spoken candidly about the challenges she and her family have faced under the constant glare of the public eye. Pinkett Smith has stressed the importance of setting boundaries, protecting one's privacy, and not allowing public opinion to dictate personal choices. She has advocated for living authentically and remaining true to oneself, regardless of outside judgments.

Despite the constant scrutiny, Pinkett Smith has used her platform to address social issues, promote positivity, and empower others. She has been open about her own struggles with mental health, sharing her experiences to reduce stigma and encourage conversations around these important topics. Pinkett Smith has also been an outspoken advocate for racial equality and women's rights, using her influence to raise awareness and inspire change.

It's worth noting that while public figures like Pinkett Smith may be subject to intense scrutiny, it is essential to remember that they are entitled to privacy and personal boundaries just like anyone else. The invasion of privacy and the perpetuation of rumors and gossip can have a significant impact on a person's mental well-being.

Pinkett Smith has faced substantial public scrutiny regarding her personal life throughout her career. From invasive rumors about her marriage to judgment regarding her personal choices, she has navigated these challenges with strength and grace. Pinkett Smith has used her platform to advocate for authenticity, set boundaries, and speak out on important social issues. Despite the scrutiny she has faced, she continues to remain resilient, true to herself, and an influential voice for positive change.

Criticism and Backlash in Hollywood

She has faced her fair share of criticism and backlash over the years like many actors in Hollywood. As a successful and influential figure in the entertainment industry, her choices, opinions, and public statements have often been subject to scrutiny and debate. Let's explore some of the criticisms and backlash that Pinkett Smith has encountered and how she has navigated these challenges.

One aspect of criticism that Pinkett Smith has faced relates to her acting career. Some critics have questioned her acting abilities and whether she has been able to maintain consistent success throughout her career. However, it is important to note that Pinkett Smith has been involved in a range of projects and has received critical acclaim for her performances in films such as "Set It Off" (1996) and "Ali" (2001). Moreover, she has demonstrated versatility and skill across various genres and platforms, including film, television, and theater.

Pinkett Smith has also encountered backlash and criticism regarding her involvement in certain films or roles. There have been discussions about cultural appropriation, with some arguing that she participated in projects that perpetuated harmful stereotypes or appropriated elements of different cultures. In response, Pinkett Smith has addressed these concerns openly and acknowledged the importance of diversity and accurate representation in the entertainment industry.

Another major instance of criticism and controversy surrounding Pinkett Smith occurred in 2016 when she and her husband, Will Smith, publicly expressed discontent with the lack of diversity in the nominations for the Academy Awards that year. They initiated a boycott of the ceremony, which garnered both support and backlash from different parts of the industry and the public. This controversy sparked important conversations about representation and diversity in Hollywood, highlighting the need for increased opportunities for underrepresented groups.

She has consistently responded to criticism and backlash with resilience and grace. Rather than allowing negative comments to deter her, she has used her platform to advocate for change, diversity, and inclusivity in the entertainment industry. Through her production company, Westbrook Studios, she has actively worked to uplift marginalized voices and promote projects that celebrate diverse perspectives.

It is important to acknowledge that criticism and backlash are an unfortunate reality for many public figures, and everyone has the right to express differing opinions. Pinkett Smith has demonstrated her willingness to engage in constructive dialogue, address concerns, and amplify important conversations that promote positive change within the industry.

Pinkett Smith has encountered criticism and backlash throughout her career in Hollywood. From questioning her acting abilities to concerns about her involvement in certain projects or roles, she has faced various challenges. However, Pinkett Smith has consistently responded with resilience, using her platform to advocate for diversity, inclusion, and positive change in the industry. By addressing controversies and engaging in meaningful conversations, she continues to make a significant impact in Hollywood and beyond.

Red Table Talk Series

"Red Table Talk" is a groundbreaking talk show hosted by Jada Pinkett Smith, her daughter Willow Smith, and her mother Adrienne Banfield-Norris. The series, which premiered on Facebook Watch in 2018, has quickly become a cultural phenomenon, known for its raw and honest conversations about a wide range of topics.

What sets "Red Table Talk" apart from other talk shows is its commitment to authenticity and vulnerability. Jada, Willow, and Adrienne create a safe space where they can openly discuss their own experiences, as well as invite guests to share their stories. The show tackles subjects such as mental health, relationships, race, and self-empowerment with a level of depth and honesty rarely seen on television.

One of the key aspects of "Red Table Talk" is its focus on intergenerational dialogue. Jada, Willow, and Adrienne come from different generations and bring their unique perspectives to the table. This dynamic allows for a rich exploration of various topics, as they navigate the complexities of their own relationships and experiences.

The show has featured a diverse range of guests, including celebrities like Demi Moore, Jordyn Woods, and Alicia Keys, as well as everyday people with extraordinary stories. Each episode is carefully crafted to provide a platform for individuals to share their truths and offer insights that can resonate with viewers around the world.

Through "Red Table Talk," Jada Pinkett Smith has created a space for open dialogue and healing. The show has become a source of inspiration and empowerment for countless viewers who find solace in knowing that they are not alone in their struggles. The conversations on the show often delve into difficult and uncomfortable topics, but they always aim to foster understanding and growth.

In addition to its impact on viewers, "Red Table Talk" has also been recognized for its philanthropic efforts. The show has partnered with various charitable organizations to raise awareness and funds for causes such as mental health, domestic violence, and racial justice.

"Red Table Talk" is a testament to Jada Pinkett Smith's commitment to using her platform for good. Through her vulnerability and willingness to address taboo subjects, she has created a show that encourages empathy, understanding, and personal growth. The series has undoubtedly left an indelible mark on the talk show landscape and continues to inspire audiences worldwide.

Overcoming Personal Struggles and Setbacks

She has faced personal struggles and setbacks throughout her life, but she has demonstrated immense resilience and the ability to overcome challenges. Her journey is a testament to her strength and determination. Let's delve into some of the personal struggles and setbacks she has encountered and how she has managed to grow and persevere.

One significant personal struggle that Pinkett Smith has openly discussed is her battle with mental health issues, particularly anxiety. She has shared that anxiety has been a constant presence in her life, affecting her well-being and relationships. Pinkett Smith has been transparent about seeking help and actively working on her mental health, emphasizing the importance of self-care and mental well-being. By speaking out about her struggles and advocating for mental health awareness, she has encouraged others to prioritize their own mental well-being and seek support when needed.

Another setback Pinkett Smith faced was her experience with addiction. She has revealed that she battled addiction in the past, specifically with alcohol and drug abuse. Overcoming addiction is a challenging and ongoing process, but Pinkett Smith made the decision to prioritize her recovery and work towards a healthier life. Through therapy, self-reflection, and a strong support system, she has been able to overcome her addiction and continue on a path of personal growth and well-being.

In her marriage to actor Will Smith, Pinkett Smith has also faced challenges and setbacks. Like any long-term relationship, they have experienced ups and downs over the years. Rumors and scrutiny surrounding their marriage have put strain on their relationship. However, Pinkett Smith has been open about the work they have done as a couple to strengthen their bond and navigate through difficult times. She emphasizes the importance of communication, trust, and constant effort to maintain a healthy and fulfilling marriage.

Furthermore, Pinkett Smith has confronted societal expectations and stereotypes, grappling with the pressure to conform to certain ideals. As an influential figure in the public eye, she has pushed back against societal expectations regarding beauty standards, gender roles, and success. Pinkett Smith has encouraged both herself and others to embrace authenticity, self-acceptance, and the courage to stay true to one's values and individuality.

Throughout these personal struggles and setbacks, Pinkett Smith has exhibited resilience and the determination to grow and overcome. She has actively sought help, engaged in self-reflection, and shared her experiences to inspire and support others facing similar challenges. Pinkett Smith's journey serves as a reminder that setbacks can be stepping stones to personal growth and that it's possible to emerge stronger and wiser from adversity.

Pinkett Smith has overcome personal struggles and setbacks by embracing vulnerability, seeking support, and prioritizing her well-being. Her journey highlights the importance of mental health, self-care, and the resilience necessary to navigate life's challenges. By sharing her experiences, she has become an empowering figure, demonstrating that setbacks can be transformed into opportunities for growth and personal transformation.

JADA PINKETT SMITH BIO

CHAPTER 8

Influence on African-American Representation in Media

The African-American in the entertainment industry is being greatly represented by Pinkett Smith. She has been using her platform and voice to advocate for greater diversity, inclusion, and opportunities for people of color. As an accomplished actress, producer, and activist, she has played a pivotal role in challenging stereotypes, promoting authentic storytelling, and amplifying underrepresented voices. Let's explore her impact on African-American representation in more detail.

One of the ways Pinkett Smith has contributed to African-American representation is through her work in film and television. Throughout her career, she has taken on roles that defy stereotypes and showcase complex, multidimensional characters. She has been involved in projects that illuminate the experiences and perspectives of African-Americans, bringing authenticity and depth to the stories being told on screen.

Moreover, Pinkett Smith has been a vocal advocate for increased opportunities and visibility for African-American artists and professionals in the industry. She has spoken out against systemic biases and the lack of diversity in Hollywood, addressing the underrepresentation of people of color in both on-screen roles and behind-the-scenes positions. By amplifying these issues, Pinkett Smith has helped spark important conversations and incite change within the industry.

Pinkett Smith's influence extends beyond her own acting career. Alongside her husband Will Smith, she founded their production company, Overbrook Entertainment, which has been dedicated to supporting diverse talent and sharing a wide range of stories that reflect different backgrounds and experiences. Under her leadership, the company has actively sought out and nurtured projects that center on African-American narratives, creating opportunities for underrepresented voices in the industry.

Additionally, Pinkett Smith has used her platform to provide opportunities for emerging talent of color. Through initiatives like the short film showcase "Project Cre8," she has facilitated access to mentorship and resources for aspiring filmmakers, particularly those from marginalized communities. By fostering an environment that nurtures and uplifts diverse voices, Pinkett Smith has played a role in cultivating the next generation of African-American storytellers.

Beyond the entertainment industry, Pinkett Smith has been an influential advocate for broader social issues affecting African-Americans. Her Facebook Watch show, "Red Table Talk," has covered a range of topics, including racism, mental health, and social justice, providing a platform for open and honest conversations. By engaging in these discussions, Pinkett Smith has helped bring attention to the experiences and challenges faced by African-Americans, contributing to a larger dialogue on racial equality and representation.

Pinkett Smith has made a significant impact on African-American representation within the entertainment industry. Through her acting career, production company, advocacy work, and initiatives supporting emerging talent, she has elevated the voices and stories of African-Americans. Pinkett Smith's dedication to challenging stereotypes, promoting diversity, and amplifying underrepresented voices has helped pave the way for a more inclusive and equitable industry. Her influence extends beyond her own success, as she has actively worked to create pathways and opportunities for future generations of African-American artists and professionals.

Contributions to Feminism and Intersectionality

The American actress and activist, has made significant contributions to feminism and intersectionality throughout her career. She is known for using her platform to advocate for gender equality, racial justice, and the empowerment of marginalized communities.

One of Pinkett Smith's notable contributions to feminism is her vocal support for women's rights. She has consistently emphasized the importance of women's voices being heard and respected. Through her work, she encourages women to embrace their power and challenge societal norms that limit their potential. Pinkett Smith has been a strong advocate for equal pay, reproductive rights, and the inclusion of women in traditionally male-dominated industries.

Intersectionality is another area where Pinkett Smith has made a significant impact. She recognizes that gender inequality intersects with other forms of oppression, such as racism and classism. Pinkett Smith uses her platform to shed light on the experiences of Black women and other marginalized groups who face multiple layers of discrimination. By highlighting the intersections of various identities and advocating for inclusive feminism, she promotes a more comprehensive understanding of social justice.

In 2018, Pinkett Smith launched a web talk show called "Red Table Talk," which has become a powerful platform for discussing important social issues. The show features honest and open conversations about topics such as mental health, relationships, and systemic injustice. Through "Red Table Talk," Pinkett Smith creates a safe space for dialogue and encourages empathy and understanding.

Her commitment to feminism and intersectionality extends beyond her professional life. Alongside her husband, Will Smith, she founded the Will and Jada Smith Family Foundation, which focuses on supporting underserved communities and promoting education and empowerment. The foundation has funded initiatives that address issues such as poverty, youth development, and access to quality education.

Furthermore, Pinkett Smith has been actively involved in organizations like the Women's March, which advocates for women's rights and social justice. She has used her voice to amplify the experiences and concerns of marginalized communities, emphasizing the need for intersectional activism.

Jada Pinkett Smith has been a prominent advocate for feminism and intersectionality. Through her work in the entertainment industry, her talk show, and her philanthropic efforts, she has consistently championed gender equality, highlighted the intersections of various forms of oppression, and worked towards creating a more inclusive and just society. Pinkett Smith's contributions have been instrumental in raising awareness and inspiring change, making her an influential figure in the feminist and intersectional movements.

Cultural Impact and Popularity

Jada has had a significant cultural impact and has become a highly popular figure in the entertainment industry. Her talent, charisma, and dedication to social justice have endeared her to audiences around the world.

One aspect of Pinkett Smith's cultural impact is her influence on fashion and style. She is known for her bold and unique fashion choices, often pushing boundaries and setting trends. Her red carpet appearances are eagerly anticipated, with fans and fashion enthusiasts eagerly awaiting her next ensemble. Pinkett Smith's fashion sense has inspired many, and she has been recognized as a style icon.

In addition to her fashion influence, Pinkett Smith's cultural impact can be seen through her roles in film and television. She has portrayed strong, independent, and complex female characters, challenging stereotypes and showcasing the depth of women's experiences. Her performances in films such as "Set It Off," "The Matrix Reloaded," and "Girls Trip" have resonated with audiences and have contributed to her popularity.

Furthermore, Pinkett Smith's cultural impact extends beyond her acting career. Her openness and vulnerability on her talk show, "Red Table Talk," have struck a chord with viewers. The show's honest discussions about personal struggles, relationships, and societal issues have made it a hit, attracting millions of viewers and sparking important conversations. Pinkett Smith's ability to connect with people on a personal level has contributed to her popularity and influence.

Pinkett Smith's cultural impact also stems from her activism and advocacy work. Her commitment to feminism, intersectionality, and social justice has resonated with many individuals who admire her dedication to creating a more equitable society. By using her platform to amplify marginalized voices and shed light on important issues, she has inspired others to take action and make a difference.

Moreover, Pinkett Smith's cultural impact can be seen in her philanthropic efforts. Through the Will and Jada Smith Family Foundation, she has supported numerous initiatives that aim to uplift underserved communities and provide opportunities for education and empowerment. Her commitment to giving back and making a positive impact on society has further solidified her cultural influence.

Overall, Jada Pinkett Smith's cultural impact and popularity can be attributed to her talent, activism, and relatability. She has used her platform to challenge societal norms, advocate for marginalized communities, and inspire others to create change. Through her fashion choices, film and television roles, talk show, and philanthropy, Pinkett Smith has become a beloved figure who has left an indelible mark on popular culture.

CHAPTER 9

WORKS, AWARDS AND RECOGNITION

Bibliography

- *"Girls Trip" (2017)* - Directed by Malcolm D. Lee, this comedy film follows four friends who travel to New Orleans for the Essence Music Festival. Pinkett Smith plays the role of Lisa Cooper, a single mother and nurse who is looking to let loose and have some fun.

- *"Set It Off" (1996)* - Directed by F. Gary Gray, this crime thriller tells the story of four women who turn to robbing banks in order to escape their difficult lives. Pinkett Smith portrays the character of Lida "Stony" Newsom, a determined and loyal friend who becomes the leader of the group.

- *"The Matrix Reloaded" (2003) and "The Matrix Revolutions" (2003)* - Directed by the Wachowski Brothers, these science fiction action films are sequels to "The Matrix." Pinkett Smith plays the role of Niobe, a skilled pilot and captain of the Logos spaceship.

- *"Ali" (2001)* - Directed by Michael Mann, this biographical sports drama follows the life and career of boxer Muhammad Ali. Pinkett Smith portrays Sonji Roi, Ali's first wife, who challenges societal expectations and fights for her own independence.

- *"Collateral" (2004)* - Directed by Michael Mann, this neo-noir crime thriller stars Tom Cruise as a contract killer who forces a taxi driver, played by Jamie Foxx, to drive him around Los Angeles. Pinkett Smith appears in a supporting role as Annie Farrell, a prosecutor who becomes involved in the dangerous situation.

Filmography

> *"A Different World" (1991-1993)* - This television sitcom is a spin-off of "The Cosby Show" and follows the lives of students at a historically Black college. Pinkett Smith appears in a recurring role as Lena James, a free-spirited and outspoken student.

> *"Gotham" (2014-2019)* - This crime drama television series is based on characters from the Batman franchise. Pinkett Smith portrays the character of Fish Mooney, a ruthless and manipulative crime boss.

> *"Hawthorne" (2009-2011)* - This medical drama television series stars Pinkett Smith as Christina Hawthorne, a Chief Nursing Officer who navigates the challenges of the healthcare system while advocating for her patients.

> *"The Nutty Professor" (1996)* - Directed by Tom Shadyac, this comedy film stars Eddie Murphy as a professor who invents a potion that transforms him into a slim and confident man. Pinkett Smith appears in a supporting role as Carla Purty, a student who becomes romantically involved with the transformed professor.

> *"Madagascar" franchise (2005-2012)* - Pinkett Smith lends her voice to the character of Gloria, a female

hippopotamus, in this animated film series about a group of zoo animals who find themselves stranded in the wild.

This bibliography and filmography provide an overview of Jada Pinkett Smith's notable works in film and television. Her diverse range of roles showcases her versatility as an actress and her ability to bring depth and authenticity to her performances. From comedic roles to dramatic portrayals, Pinkett Smith has made a significant impact on the entertainment industry.

Awards and Nominations

As an accomplished actress, producer, and businesswoman, Jada Pinkett Smith has received recognition and acclaim for her contributions to the entertainment industry. As a result of this, she has an impressive list of awards and nominations that highlight her talent and versatility. Let's delve into Jada Pinkett Smith's notable accolades.

Jada Pinkett Smith's awards journey began in 1997 when she received her first nomination for the NAACP Image Award for Outstanding Supporting Actress in a Motion Picture for her role in "Set It Off." She went on to win the award in 2005 for her performance in "Collateral." Throughout her career, she has been honored with multiple NAACP Image Awards, including Outstanding Actress in a Motion Picture for "The Matrix Reloaded" (2004) and "The Matrix Revolutions" (2004).

In 2002, Pinkett Smith was nominated for the Black Reel Award for Best Supporting Actress for her portrayal of Sonji Roi, the first wife of Muhammad Ali, in the biographical drama "Ali." Her exceptional performance in this film also earned her a nomination for the BET Award for Best Actress.

Pinkett Smith's talent and dedication have been recognized by various award organizations. In 2009, she received a nomination for the Critics' Choice Television Award for Best Supporting Actress in a Drama Series for her role as Christina Hawthorne in the medical drama series "Hawthorne." She also earned a nomination for the Teen Choice Award for Choice TV Actress: Drama.

In addition to acting, Pinkett Smith has made significant contributions as a producer. She co-produced the biographical drama film "The Secret Life of Bees" (2008), which garnered several award nominations, including the NAACP Image Award for Outstanding Motion Picture. She also served as an executive producer for the critically acclaimed film "Fences" (2016), which received numerous accolades, including Academy Award nominations for Best Picture and Best Adapted Screenplay.

Pinkett Smith's work as a producer extended to television as well. She co-created and executive produced the talk show "Red Table Talk" alongside her daughter Willow Smith and mother Adrienne Banfield-Norris. The show has received widespread acclaim and has been nominated for several awards, including the Critics' Choice Real TV Award for Best Talk Show.

Beyond her professional achievements, Pinkett Smith has also been recognized for her philanthropic efforts. In 2012, she was honored with the Power of Women Award at the Essence Black Women in Hollywood Luncheon for her work with the organization DonorsChoose.org.

While Jada Pinkett Smith may not have a discography, her numerous awards and nominations speak to her talent, versatility, and contributions to the entertainment industry. Her ability to captivate audiences through her performances and her dedication to producing meaningful content have solidified her status as a respected figure in Hollywood.

In conclusion, Jada Pinkett Smith's life history is a testament to her immense talent, versatility, and dedication to the entertainment industry. From her early beginnings as an actress to her successful forays into producing and philanthropy, Pinkett Smith has consistently proven herself as a force to be reckoned with.

Her impressive list of awards and nominations, including multiple NAACP Image Awards, Black Reel Awards, and Critics' Choice Television Award nominations, showcases her ability to captivate audiences and deliver exceptional performances. Whether it be her roles in films such as "Set It Off," "Ali," or the "Matrix" trilogy, Pinkett Smith has consistently displayed her range and skill as an actress.

Furthermore, Pinkett Smith's contributions as a producer have been equally noteworthy. Her involvement in films like "The Secret Life of Bees" and "Fences" demonstrate her commitment to telling meaningful stories and bringing important narratives to the forefront. Additionally, her work as a co-creator and executive producer of the talk show "Red Table Talk" has allowed her to connect with audiences on a deeper level and address important topics with authenticity and vulnerability.

Beyond her professional accomplishments, Pinkett Smith's philanthropic efforts have also made a significant impact. Her work with organizations like DonorsChoose.org has earned her recognition and praise for her dedication to making a difference in the lives of others.

Overall, Jada Pinkett Smith's life history is one of remarkable achievements and contributions. Her talent, versatility, and commitment to creating meaningful content have solidified her status as a respected figure in Hollywood. As she continues to evolve and make her mark on the entertainment industry, it is clear that Pinkett Smith's legacy will endure for years to come.

CONCLUSION

Enduring Influence

Jada Pinkett Smith's enduring influence can be seen in various aspects of her career and personal life. From her impact on fashion and style to her roles in film and television, her talk show, activism, and philanthropy, Pinkett Smith has left a lasting mark on popular culture.

One of the most notable aspects of Pinkett Smith's enduring influence is her fashion sense. Throughout her career, she has consistently made bold and unique fashion choices that have set trends and pushed boundaries. Her red carpet appearances are eagerly anticipated, with fans and fashion enthusiasts eagerly awaiting her next ensemble. Pinkett Smith's fearlessness in experimenting with different styles and her ability to effortlessly pull off any look have established her as a style icon. Her influence can be seen in the way many people now approach fashion with a sense of individuality and self-expression.

In addition to her fashion influence, Pinkett Smith's impact can be seen through her roles in film and television. She has consistently portrayed strong, independent, and complex female characters that challenge stereotypes and showcase the depth of women's experiences. Her performances in films such as "Set It Off," where she played a bank robber seeking justice, "The Matrix Reloaded," where she portrayed a skilled fighter, and "Girls Trip," where she showcased the joys and challenges of female friendship, have resonated with audiences and have contributed to her popularity. Pinkett Smith's ability to bring depth and authenticity to her characters has made her a highly respected and sought-after actress.

Furthermore, Pinkett Smith's cultural impact extends beyond her acting career. Her talk show, "Red Table Talk," has become a phenomenon, attracting millions of viewers and sparking important conversations. The show's success can be attributed to Pinkett Smith's openness and vulnerability as she discusses personal struggles, relationships, and societal issues. Through these honest discussions, she has created a safe space for viewers to engage with difficult topics and reflect on their own lives. Pinkett Smith's ability to connect with people on a personal level and her commitment to promoting empathy and understanding have made "Red Table Talk" a platform for healing and growth.

Pinkett Smith's enduring influence also stems from her activism and advocacy work. She has been a vocal advocate for feminism, intersectionality, and social justice, using her platform to amplify marginalized voices and shed light on important issues. Pinkett Smith's dedication to creating a more equitable society has inspired many individuals who admire her commitment to making a difference. By speaking out and taking action, she has encouraged others to do the same and has sparked conversations that challenge the status quo.

Moreover, Pinkett Smith's philanthropic efforts have further solidified her cultural influence. Through the Will and Jada Smith Family Foundation, she has supported numerous initiatives that aim to uplift underserved communities and provide opportunities for education and empowerment. Her commitment to giving back and making a positive impact on society has not only contributed to her popularity but has also inspired others to get involved in philanthropy and contribute to the greater good.

In conclusion, Jada Pinkett Smith's enduring influence can be attributed to her talent, activism, and relatability. Her impact can be seen in her fashion choices, film and television roles, talk show, activism, and philanthropy. Pinkett Smith has used her platform to challenge societal norms, advocate for marginalized communities, and inspire others to create change. Her cultural influence is a testament to her ability to connect with people on a personal level and her unwavering dedication to making a positive impact on the world.

Reflection on Achievements and Contributions

Jada Pinkett Smith has reflected on her achievements and contributions throughout her career, recognizing the impact she has had on various aspects of popular culture and society as a whole. She acknowledges that her fashion choices have pushed boundaries and inspired others to embrace their individuality and self-expression. Pinkett Smith takes pride in being a style icon and recognizes the influence she has had in shaping trends and challenging conventional fashion norms.

In terms of her roles in film and television, Pinkett Smith reflects on the strong and complex female characters she has portrayed. She recognizes the importance of these characters in challenging stereotypes and showcasing the depth of women's experiences. Pinkett Smith takes pride in bringing authenticity and depth to her performances, knowing that her portrayals have resonated with audiences and contributed to her success as an actress.

Pinkett Smith also reflects on the success of her talk show, "Red Table Talk," and the impact it has had on viewers. She acknowledges the power of vulnerability and openness in creating a safe space for important conversations. Pinkett Smith is proud that the show has provided a platform for healing and growth, allowing viewers to engage with difficult topics and reflect on their own lives. She recognizes the impact of her personal stories and discussions on relationships, struggles, and societal issues, knowing that they have sparked important conversations and encouraged empathy and understanding.

As an activist, Pinkett Smith reflects on her dedication to feminism, intersectionality, and social justice. She acknowledges the importance of using her platform to amplify marginalized voices and shed light on important issues. Pinkett Smith takes pride in challenging the status quo and inspiring others to speak out and take action. She recognizes that her activism has sparked conversations and encouraged individuals to make a difference in their own communities.

Furthermore, Pinkett Smith reflects on her philanthropic efforts and the impact they have had on underserved communities. She acknowledges the importance of giving back and providing opportunities for education and empowerment. Pinkett Smith takes pride in her commitment to making a positive impact on society and recognizes that her philanthropy has inspired others to get involved and contribute to the greater good.

Overall, Jada Pinkett Smith reflects on her achievements and contributions with a sense of pride and gratitude. She recognizes the influence she has had on fashion, film and television, talk show hosting, activism, and philanthropy. Pinkett Smith acknowledges the power of her platform and the importance of using it to challenge norms, advocate for marginalized communities, and inspire others to create change. Her reflection on her accomplishments serves as a reminder of the impact one person can have on the world when they are dedicated to making a positive difference.

Conclusion

Jada Pinkett Smith's life history and career achievements have been characterized by immense talent, versatility, and a commitment to using her platform to inspire and uplift others. As we reach the conclusion of her remarkable journey, it is evident that she has left an indelible mark on the entertainment industry and beyond. Let's explore an extensive and fitting conclusion that captures the essence of Jada Pinkett Smith's extraordinary life and career.

> ➤ *A Life of Creativity and Empowerment*

Jada Pinkett Smith's life has been a testament to the power of creativity, resilience, and empowerment. From her early days as a budding actress to her multifaceted accomplishments as an artist, producer, and philanthropist, Pinkett Smith has consistently pushed boundaries and shattered glass ceilings.

Throughout her career, Pinkett Smith has demonstrated an immense range as an actress, fearlessly taking on diverse roles that showcase her immense talent. Whether portraying strong-willed characters in films such as "Set It Off" and "Ali," or bringing warmth and wisdom to her mesmerizing performances in "The Nutty Professor" and "The Matrix" trilogy, Pinkett Smith's versatility has captivated audiences and critics alike.

Beyond her work on screen, Pinkett Smith's contributions as a producer and advocate for representation and diversity have been groundbreaking. Through her production company, Overbrook Entertainment, Pinkett Smith has championed projects that challenge societal norms and amplify marginalized voices. From her involvement in the hit show "Gotham" to the groundbreaking series "Red Table Talk," Pinkett Smith has demonstrated her commitment to telling stories that inspire dialogue, foster understanding, and effect lasting social change.

> ## *A Voice of Empowerment and Authenticity*

Pinkett Smith's impact extends beyond the entertainment industry. She has used her platform to raise awareness about important social issues, promote mental health and well-being, and empower individuals to embrace their authentic selves. Through her candid and introspective discussions on "Red Table Talk," Pinkett Smith has created a space where vulnerability is celebrated, difficult conversations are had, and empathy is fostered. Her willingness to share her own experiences and challenges has allowed others to find solace and support.

As an advocate for women's rights and empowerment, Pinkett Smith has been unwavering in her commitment to uplifting and inspiring women around the world. Through her philanthropic efforts and engagement with various organizations, she has worked to shatter stereotypes and promote inclusivity, opening doors for future generations of women in the entertainment industry and beyond.

> ## *A Lasting Legacy*

Jada Pinkett Smith's legacy is one of resilience, authenticity, and empowerment. Her remarkable journey in the entertainment industry has demonstrated her unwavering dedication to her craft, her commitment to using her platform for positive change, and her ability to spark important conversations. As a trailblazer and role model, Pinkett Smith has left an indelible mark on the lives of millions, inspiring individuals to embrace their own uniqueness and pursue their passions with unwavering determination.

Looking towards the future, it is clear that Jada Pinkett Smith's impact will continue to resonate for generations to come. Her influence as an artist, producer, advocate, and pillar of empowerment will continue to shape the entertainment industry and inspire individuals to live authentic lives filled with purpose and compassion.

In conclusion, Jada Pinkett Smith's life history and career achievements affirm her status as a true icon. Through her remarkable contributions on screen, behind the scenes, and in empowering others, Pinkett Smith has demonstrated the transformative power of leveraging one's platform to create positive change. Her legacy as a multifaceted artist, trailblazer, and advocate for authenticity and empowerment is a testament to her incredible journey, and it will forever inspire and uplift those who follow her footsteps.

Printed in Great Britain
by Amazon

31411866R00046